4.93
10.13.08
cmn-J

W9-AVR-516

Skunks

by **Steven Otfinoski**

Marshall Cavendish
Benchmark
New York

Thanks to Jerry W. Dragoo, Ph.D., Mephitologist and Research Associate,
Division of Mammals, Museum of Southwestern Biology, University of New Mexico,
for his expert reading of this manuscript.

Marshall Cavendish Benchmark
99 White Plains Road
Tarrytown, New York 10591-5502
www.marshallcavendish.us

Text copyright © 2009 by Marshall Cavendish Corporation

All Web sites were available and accurate when sent to press.

Library of Congress Cataloging-in-Publication Data

Otfinoski, Steven.
Skunks / by Steven Otfinoski.
p. cm. —(Animals animals)
Summary: "Provides comprehensive information on the anatomy, special skills, habitats,
and diet of skunks"—Provided by publisher.
Includes index.
ISBN 978-0-7614-2929-6
1. Skunks—Juvenile literature. I. Title.

QL737.C248O84 2008
599.76'8—dc22

2007024117

Photo research by Joan Meisel

Cover photo: Tim Fitzharris/Minden Pictures

The photographs in this book are used by permission and through the courtesy of:
Alamy: Papilio, 7; Ruth Hoyt, 31; Visuals&Written SL, 32; Jochen Tack, 38; Transtock Inc., 40. *Animals Animals -
Earth Scenes*: Gordon & Cathy ILLG, 16; Erwin & Peggy Bauer, 25, 28. *Bruce Coleman Inc.*: John Ebeling, 6.
Corbis: Tom Brakefield, 4; D. Robert & Lorri Franz, 12, 22; Michael DeYoung, 26, 36; John Conrad, 34.
Getty Images: Thomas Kitchin & Victoria Hurst, 1. *Minden Pictures*: Claus Meyer, 9; Tim Fitzharris, 30.
Peter Arnold, Inc.: Bruce Lichtenberger, 18. *Photo Researchers, Inc.*: Stephen J. Krasemann, 10; Anthony Mercieca, 11;
Leonard Lee Rue lll, 14; E.R. Degginger, 19; Steve Maslowski, 20. *SuperStock*: age fotostock, 24.

Editor: Joy Bean
Publisher: Michelle Bisson
Art Director: Anahid Hamparian
Series Designer: Adam Mietlowski

Printed in Malaysia
654321

Contents

1 The Smell That Stays

A large dog sights an intruder in its backyard one night. A small, furry creature is waddling toward the woods. The dog starts to bark and chase after it. The animal quickens its pace, but the dog is faster. Then the animal stops and turns. It lifts its long, bushy tail. It hisses and growls at the dog. It flashes sharp teeth, but the dog is not afraid. It has sharp teeth too. The small animal begins to stamp both front feet on the ground. The dog finds this rather amusing. Finally, the animal twists its rear end around, its long bushy tail still in the air. The dog is quite fascinated and runs closer. Suddenly the animal sprays a cloud of liquid that the dog runs into. Some of it lands in the

When a skunk feels threatened, its tail goes up and it sprays musk at its enemy.

5

This dog is looking for a fight, and may soon be sprayed.

Did You Know . . .

The word *skunk* comes from a Native American word that means "one who sprays."

dog's eyes and stings them. The dog howls. It cannot see. Most of the liquid lands on its fur and burns right through to the skin. The blindness will soon go away and so will the burning, but the awful smell will stay on the poor dog for days. Still howling, the dog runs for home. It has learned an important lesson—you do not mess with a striped skunk!

6

The white stripes on a skunk's back are a distinguishing feature, so other animals know to stay away.

Species Chart

◆ The striped skunk is the most common skunk in the United States. It has black fur and white stripes that run from its tiny head to the end of its long tail. No two striped skunks have the exact same stripe pattern. It is 13 to 18 inches (33 to 46 centimeters) in length without its tail, about the size of a house cat. It weighs between 6 and 14 pounds (2.7 to 6.3 kilograms). It lives in North America from central Canada to northern Mexico.

◆ The hog-nosed skunk got its peculiar name from its large nose, which looks like a pig's snout. It uses its nose to root out of the ground its favorite food—insects. It weighs about the same as the striped skunk but is bigger, between 20 and 36 inches (50 and 91 cm). The hog-nosed skunk lives in the southwestern United States and Central America and is the only skunk found in South America.

The hog-nosed skunk.

The western spotted skunk.

◆ The eastern and western spotted skunks are the smallest skunks. They have white spots on their black fur instead of stripes. They are the only skunks that can climb trees. The western spotted skunk lives in the western United States, Mexico, and Central America. The eastern spotted skunk can be found south of Canada to Mexico, Florida, the Appalachians, and Pennsylvania. The southern spotted skunk can be found from Central Mexico to Costa Rica.

◆ The hooded skunk got its name from the long hairs around its neck, which resembles a hood. Its tail can grow to 16 inches (41 cm) in length—the longest tail, compared to body size, of any skunk. It is found in temperate and tropical habitats from the southwestern United States to Costa Rica.

The hooded skunk.

While the odor a skunk can leave behind is large, the skunk itself is a small animal.

The skunk is armed with one of the most powerful defense weapons in nature—an oily yellow liquid called *musk* that it squirts at enemies from the two walnut-size *glands* on either side of its *anus*. The dog in the scene above ignored all the skunk's warnings, forcing the skunk to use its ultimate weapon. The dog also missed a visual warning—the two long white stripes down the skunk's black, furry back. It is a sign to other animals to stay away.

There are six *species* of skunks in North America. Of the twelve species worldwide, ten are found only in the Western Hemisphere. The North American skunk species are the striped skunk, the hog-nosed skunk, the western spotted skunk, the eastern spotted skunk, the southern spotted skunk, and the hooded skunk. Skunks have rather long bodies, small heads, and short, muscular legs. They usually move slowly, but when being chased by another animal, skunks can run at up to 10 miles (16.1 kilometers) per hour for short distances. Each of the skunk's four feet has five partially webbed toes, and each toe has a sharp, curved claw. The skunk uses its front claws to dig up insects living in the ground. It also has sharp teeth that it uses to bite and kill larger *prey*.

The eastern spotted skunk looks similar to the western spotted skunk,
but can only be found in the eastern part of the United States.

The skunk has two layers of fur. The outer layer has very long hairs that keep out rain and snow. The inner layer has short, kinky hairs. They act as insulation to keep in its body heat and keep out the winter cold.

A Shy Creature

Skunks are shy and gentle creatures. Males usually live alone while females live with their babies. Adult skunks only come together during the mating season. Skunks usually live in grassy areas, woodlands, and meadows, although they are very adaptable. They have been known to live in developed areas. Skunks usually live within 2 miles (3.2 km) of water. Their homes are called *dens*. Sometimes they dig out their own dens. Other times they move into dens abandoned by other animals or find natural dens, such as hollow logs. The spotted skunk can climb and will often make its home in the hollow part of a tree. In populated areas, skunks may even live in barns or

A mother skunk takes care of her babies until they are ready to venture out on their own.

Skunks can live in a variety of places, but a favorite is in hollow logs.

under houses. Wherever their dens might be, skunks line them with dry leaves and grass to keep them warm in winter.

Skunks are *nocturnal* animals. That means they sleep in the daytime and are active at night. In the winter, when food is

18

scarce, skunks may sleep both day and night for a long time. But unlike other animals, they do not *hibernate* all winter. They will wake up when the weather is warmer and go out to hunt for food. Then they will return to their dens for another long nap.

This striped skunk is resting after a full night of hunting for food.

Did You Know . . .
A skunk will sneeze not because it has a cold but to clear out its nose so it can better smell plant food or animal prey.

Skunks have an appetite for a number of different kinds of food, including the eggs of other animals.

Skunks are *omnivorous*. They will eat both the flesh of other animals and plants. Insects are their favorite food. But they also hunt and kill larger animals, such as mice, frogs, birds, and even rabbits. They also like the eggs of

20

turtles, snakes, and some birds. Skunks eat berries, apples, nuts, mushrooms, and a variety of other plant material.

Skunks rely on their keen senses of smell and hearing to hunt for food. As they walk along, they usually keep their noses to the earth to sniff out bugs and worms living underground. Once they find their prey, they dig them out with their sharp claws. They use their hearing to detect the sounds of moving insects or animals. Once they find where the sound is coming from, they pounce on their prey. One poorly developed sense in skunks is their eyesight. They cannot see an object clearly beyond a few feet.

3 Mates, Moms, and Kits

In February or March, skunks leave their dens and go looking for mates. Males look for females in their *territory*, which may cover 30 to 40 acres (12.1 to 16.2 hectares). Female skunks have a home range that they wander across. A male can spend days or weeks looking in one den after another for a mate. When he finds one, he might find another male skunk that also wants to mate with her. When this happens, the two males have a fight. The stronger one usually prevails, but if they reach a stalemate, they may square off for a real fight. What they almost never do is raise their tails and squirt musk at each other. Their supply of musk is limited, and they will save it for when they face a large *predator*.

A young skunk, a kit, pokes its head out of its home in a hollow log.

The mother of these baby skunks took great care building the nest.

When the winner prevails, the loser creeps away and must make his own den. The female then mates with the winner if she wants to. The male may stay around for a while after mating, but if he does not leave soon, the female will force him to do so. He is not needed to help raise the young and, in some cases, may even try to eat them!

The female builds a nest in her den. She lines it with soft grass and dead leaves. She covers the opening to her den with bundles of grass. This will help keep out the cold.

About two months after mating, the mother gives birth to four to six baby skunks, called *kits*. The kits are completely helpless at birth. They are each about 3 to 4 inches (7.6 to 10.2 cm) long and weigh about

Did You Know . . .
Kits practice raising their tails for spraying musk at an enemy, but their musk glands are not fully developed until they are about six weeks old.

All skunks are born with their identifying stripes or spots.

These young skunks are growing up and are almost ready to set out on their own.

an ounce (28.4 grams). They are blind and deaf, and they have no teeth. But the trademark of all skunks, the black-and-white pattern, is already present in the thin coat of fur on their tiny bodies.

Within half an hour after birth, the kits begin feeding on their mother's milk through her *teats*. The kits grow rapidly. Within a week they double their weight. In three weeks, they can see and hear. After about eight weeks their mother brings them live prey to eat. It is their first solid food.

At about seven or eight weeks, the kits are ready to make their first journey outside the nest. At night the mother leads her brood outdoors in single file. They look like a parade in black and white. The kits watch closely as their mother demonstrates how to catch insects and small animals. They imitate her and hunt their own food, rooting out bugs and worms from the ground.

By late summer the young skunks are ready to leave the nest and go off on their own. Each kit will find or make its own den and fatten up on food for the coming winter. When winter ends, the skunks begin to look for a mate and have kits of their own.

4 The Ultimate Weapon

The skunk has little to fear from most predators. Once a hungry animal sees its black fur and white stripes or spots it goes looking elsewhere for a meal. It knows that this is a skunk that can squirt it with a bad-smelling liquid whose odor it will carry around for days.

What is it that makes skunk musk smell so bad? Scientists have analyzed the liquid and found it to contain a potent blend of chemical compounds called *thiols*. Thiols are so powerful that the human nose can detect them at about one part per billion in the surrounding air. The smell can carry up to a mile (1.6 km). You may remember getting a whiff of skunk

With their distinct spots, other animals can see skunks from far away.

If left alone, a skunk will not have to fire its musk to protect itself.

musk while riding with your family through the countryside, even with the car windows closed.

Despite the power of its ultimate weapon, the skunk is reluctant to use it. In fact, it will only spray an intruder as a last resort, after it has tried everything else to scare it off. The warnings include foot stamping, hissing, growling, and lifting its tail. There is a good reason for the skunk's reluctance to fire its musk. Its musk glands produce only

The telltale striped tail means a skunk is likely ready to defend itself.

The great horned owl is one of the skunk's biggest predators.

about a tablespoon of musk at a time. That is good for about five squirts. Once that is used up, it takes several days for the skunk's body to refill the musk glands, although it can fire fluid before the glands are completely full.

When ready to fire, the skunk lifts its tail as high as it can. Powerful muscles surrounding the musk glands allow it to fire with great accuracy up to about 15 feet (4.6 meters) away. In the air, the spray takes on the form of a fine mist that will cling stubbornly to an animal's fur or a person's clothes.

Not all predators are scared off by a skunk's musk. Bobcats, foxes, owls, and other large predators may still attempt to attack. Of these, the skunk's greatest threat is the great horned owl. This large predator can swoop down quickly, making hardly a sound, and can seize the skunk in its *talons* before the skunk has enough time to shoot off its spray. But even if the skunk gets a chance to spray the great horned owl, it would hardly matter. Like most birds, the great horned owl has a very poor sense of smell.

If you ever have the misfortune of being sprayed by a skunk, getting rid of the stink is not easy. Washing the body with vinegar or tomato juice will

This skunk is trying to outrun its enemies.

not break up the thiols but will usually mask the smell until it fades with time. Clothing can be washed repeatedly with vinegar and baking soda and hung outside for a month. If your pet is sprayed, you can wash it with tomato juice or with over-the-counter preparations.

Skunks and People

Skunks and people get along surprisingly well. Skunks are gentle and intelligent animals that can make excellent pets. But do not try to make a pet out of a wild skunk. They must be bred as pets. You can buy and keep skunks as pets only in certain states. But first their musk glands must be removed.

There was a time, however, when skunks were hunted and killed in North America for their fur, which was made into coats and jackets. Since manufacturers did not think people would buy coats made of skunk fur, they called it "black marten" or "Alaskan sable." New laws were passed that called

Some skunks that have had their musk glands removed make good pets.

Clothing designers once used the thick fur of the skunk to make coats.

for honest labeling on clothing products, and manufacturers had to call a skunk a skunk. Sales of skunk coats plunged, and today there is little market for skunk fur.

But people are still killing skunks, although unintentionally. Half of all skunk deaths are caused by road accidents. A slow-moving skunk will start to cross a busy road at night. Because it has poor eyesight, it does not see a car zooming down the road until it is too late. According to statistics, fewer than 10 percent of skunks in the United States live longer than three years.

While most people cannot stand the smell of skunk musk, some scientists have found a useful purpose for it—to help detect natural gas leaks. Natural gas is used to heat and power some homes and buildings. But it is colorless and has no smell. When there is a leak in a pipeline or in an appliance in a home the gas cannot be noticed. It can accumulate and cause a deadly explosion. Scientists have been able to copy the skunk smell by mixing certain chemicals in a laboratory. Then they put small amounts of

Did You Know . . .
Most farmers like skunks because skunks prefer to eat insects that can destroy crops, such as crickets and grasshoppers. Scientists believe that skunks eat more insects than all other *mammals* combined.

Cars are a threat to skunks that are too slow to cross roads quickly.

this artificial "skunk juice" into natural gas before it is pumped through pipelines. Any leak in the system will be noticed immediately due to the terrible smell.

Skunks are fascinating animals that leave their mark—and smell—wherever they go.

Glossary

anus—Opening in an animal's rear from which it eliminates waste.

den—The home of an animal, often in a secluded place.

glands—Organs of an animal's body that make and give out a substance.

hibernate—To go into a deep sleep for the winter; something certain animals do to survive the cold and scarcity of food.

kits—The young of skunks or other furbearing animals.

mammal—A warm-blooded animal that has hair or fur and nurses its young with its own milk.

musk—A strong-smelling liquid produced by the glands of skunks and other animals.

nocturnal—Active during the night.

omnivorous—Eating both animals and plants.

predators—Animals that prey on, and eat, other animals to survive.

prey—An animal that is hunted and eaten by other animals.

species—Animals that share the same characteristics and mate only with their own kind.

talons—The claws of a bird of prey.

teats—The nipples of female animals through which milk flows out for its young to drink.

territory—An area that an animal lives in and defends from other animals of the same kind or species.

thiols—Chemical compounds that make up the musk of skunks and other animals.

Find Out More

Books

Greenberg, David T. *Skunks!* Boston: Little, Brown Young Readers, 2003.

Markle, Sandra. *Skunks* (Animal Prey). Minneapolis, MN: Lerner Publications, 2007.

Mason, Adrienne. *Skunks* (Kids Can Press Wildlife Series). Tonawanda, NY: Kids Can Press, Ltd., 2006.

Ziefert, Harriet. *One Smart Skunk*. Maplewood, NJ: Blue Apple Books, 2004.

Web Sites

Living with Skunks
http://www.projectwildlife.org/
living-skunks.htm

Striped Skunks
http://www.desertusa.com/
desertanimals/skunk.html

Striped Skunks—*Mephitis mephitis*
http://www.nhptv.org/natureworks/
stripedskunk.htm

Index

Page numbers for illustrations are in **boldface**.

About the Author

Steven Otfinoski is the author of numerous books about animals. He wrote five books in World Book's award-winning Animals of the World series. He has also written *Koalas*, *Sea Horses*, *Alligators*, and *Hummingbirds* in the AnimalsAnimals series. He lives in Connecticut with his wife, a high school teacher and editor.